THE LONELY RUBY

An Anthology

Taran Balakrishnan

Powered by

24by7publishing.com

This book **'The Lonely Ruby - An Anthology'** by Taran Balakrishnan is self-published by the author.

All the printing & distribution process of the book is powered by

24by7 Publishing
13 New Road, Kolkata - 51, India
https://www.24by7publishing.com
mail@24by7publishing.com
+91 9831 470 133
+91 9433 444 334

MRP: INR 199.00

First Published in February, 2024

Version 1.00

ISBN: 978-81-967781-0-1

Powered by

24by7publishing.com

Foreword

Poetry is profound in thought and diction. By careful selection of words, arranged in lyrical fashion with rhythm, syllabic beats and rhymes, good poetry evokes imagination, ignites the thinking fecundity, and the reader becomes alive to the experiences of the poet.

This is the way to describe the poetry of Taran, an avid reader, active debater, drama actor and public speaker. Multitalented and outgoing in nature, his poems are a reflection of his character – thoughtful, reflective and intense.

The water plant reed, figurative representation of the frailty of human mind, is well depicted in the poem 'As She Leeds' where the concept of 'love' or rather the 'non-existence of love' is contrasted through the two characters – 'One was all one wished to be, He who possessed every key' and 'another man passed through…he was different in a way, that made me think t'was a new day'. This poem walks us through the conflicting emotions of the 'id' and the 'super ego'. While 'id' is carried away by humanly senses and desires, super ego restraints the impulsive nature of 'id' based on practical and ethical principles.

Get a hold of your debilitating mind and move on with life is the wisely dictum in the poem 'A Stranger's Help'. Addressed to the youth of today, the poem lays threadbare the emotional upheaval of a young mind, grappling with the societal pressure and servitude of lost love. 'Thy psyche and body must wake! Thou shalt flieth thy wings and soar to free! Not more can such problems impair thy gaily self, suffer never further' is the message to the young lad, encouraging him to rise up over the turmoil of life.

Human love for a furry companion and poet's thoughtfulness about the loneliness that shall befall the canine tugs at our heart in 'My Request' whilst 'A Beggar of the Sun' is a cherished walk through the ancient Greek mythology that 2 revolves around the amorous Apollo and his unquenched love for Daphne. True to her name, Daphne is a victor in this love game. The fine tapestry of this poem paints the dainty picture of satyrs chasing the young fillies, stallions and mares in secret coves, titillating nymphs indulging in lascivious carnal love while ornate, bright and glowing Sun is defeated and dejected in love.

Yet, the Sun continues his pursuit to realize his love and enjoy its fruits in the poem 'Ayeloie', rich in nature's bounty and abundance, 'deepest green and winsome glean' as well as its fury and vehemence, 'the crops that bathe in my glory, will dry and turn to barren stalks, and grassy prairies turned to rocks, will curse your name to deepened smoke' which offer a welcoming treat for the senses. 'Cherry Butterflies is yet another poem that talks about the pain of unrequited love. 'Socrates' is a eulogy to

Socrates, the Greek philosopher from Athens, who walked this earth from 470 to 399 BC. Even today he is deemed with respect and reverence as the founder of Western Philosophy. Yet his life's chronicle tells about his trial on counts of impiety and corrupting the youth of his times. Unfair though it was, he was sentenced to death. He spent his last day in prison. Albeit the many ways to escape from captivity, with the aid of his friends and followers, he embraced death after drinking poison hemlock. This poem is a depiction of the last hours of Socrates before he succumbs to fate.

'The Avian Symphonaiae' is a royal indulgence in the many versions of opera – 'Oh, glimmer your pretty eyes; the Valla ball, the dance, concert! will take the stars and rise'. On stage, engrossed deeply in action, we saw through the poet's eyes the pirate, the blackbird, the skylark, the soldier and the whistler. The clandestine tryst between the bumblebee and fully bloomed dahlia in 'The Bee and the Dahlia' is a realistic portrayal on a lighter note, capturing the fickleness of love that runs shallow, only skin deep, and is not willing to make compromises.

'The Girl of Dragon Cove' and 'Pledin' are two poems which have a narrative pitch and both use the play of poignant undertones to convey the moral message, strong and clear. How trusting a beastly dragon led to eternal bondage is the story in the first poem while the latter, invoking the threads of Shakespearean play Macbeth, describes how Pledin's unwise advice leads to total destruction in Ambarin's kingdom.

The young poet's imaginative mind has fine - brushed in detail the world of hypocrisy through the depiction of the caves of Reld in the poem 'The Invention of the Dare'. Drinking from the goblet of hypocrisy, the world swells up in emotions of lust, greed and vanity. The play of words 'sunny night' itself shows how deceptive and unreliable is the world! Innocent men fall prey to this vicious and devious world!

‘The Maker of Fools’ is a reiteration of sanity and wisdom when superego takes control of the id, stating emphatically,

‘But rather one should wish to be
Of rich in mind and rich in heart
But such a soul is rare to see
For mind and heart do live apart’

‘The Queen’s Garden’ is a heart wrenching narrative of the sisters who steals bread to appease their hunger pangs and are subjected to torture and eventually death by slaying owing to the tyranny of the queen. It is a well - established fact that during the era of British colonization of India, their reprehensible policies of syphoning off the resources of India to Great Britain had resulted in induced famines over the course of the 18th, 19th, and early 20th centuries claiming the lives of nearly thirty million people of Indian origin. Yet, like arejuvenated phoenix, India has risen from the ashes to tell the world that our lives matter and we are unbeatable, akin to the protagonist in the poem who returns back empowered and strong - ‘tumbled through from the endless desert, the Silver-tongued God’s daughter’

Reading these poems, deliberating over the hidden meanings, understanding the style and diction in order to pen a few lines as ‘foreword’ was a great experience no doubt. Each poem in this collection has the quality of ‘call of duty’, making us think deeper, analyze more. With such philosophical concepts and poetic insights, this collection will surely entice the readers.

February, 2024 **Dr.T.Sumathy (a) Thamizhachi Thangapandian**

Member of Parliament (Lok Sabha)

South Chennai Parliamentary Constituency

Contents

The Bee and the Dahlia *(23 Nov 2022)*

All sat still on one fine day
Without a man who pass'd that way
The florets glistered in the sun
T'was beauty that met days begun

And there in this fanciful show
Of petals, stalks and mistletoe
The queen who wore her supple crown
The Dahlia, of yellow down!

From its shadows pooled a girl
Who was, as beauty goes, a pearl
And this winsome mare did sit
And sing as her heart thought it fit

Upon this sunlit morning came
A bumblebee, who sought a dame
Thus when he to this setting flew
The sight of her made his heart coo

As he fluttered close to her
His wings a soft entrancing purr
Or such he did think, at least
That his visage was quite a feast

Then, with a golden flash and sight
A dapper man out of the light
His suit sun hue, his eyes a blue
The bumblebee did turn into

And though not with a solid glance
His handsome form made her heart dance
She used the corners of her eyes
As though they bred in far eyries

With a princely bow, he sung
T'were strange, for his kind had no lung
As though the liquid that he reaped
The pretty prose from his mouth seeped

"O, Dahlia, turn up your hat
Such I may see thou face
So don't bat thou lash like a whip
That cuts across my heart
For in me you may see a lark
The contrast is not short of stark
The poultry stock sings of the sky
While I sing here to make you mine
O, droop not thou sunny drapers
And look me in all my five eyes
Do kill now your sultry tinge
And show me to your joyaunce, Ah!
Let no false unnotice plague you
And look upon me with eyes true
For I know that they caper so
And long to see the seed I sow
So speak forth what that I'm astray
For thou need not of slight ennuis
My strength is as ten men who fight
My sting doth sing a song of white"

"I see you, mast and calliday
Flatters me, this month of May!
But pretty words are scarcely fees
Though it come from a Lord of bees
The mantis offers hunted meals
A promise to which most nymphs keel
The hornet is, if nothing quite
A dashing sight and sturdy might

What say you, golden Apis?
What wins you kissed of my bliss?
Your beauty t'would like winsome birds
Matched fairly by your winsome words

What happiness is mine to take
To what end will you show your stake
The moon must know of me and you
Though many moons seen such untrue

What moneys have you for my please
What give you to buy my heart's keys
What hand dealt you for our fate
I must know, should you pollinate

I'm not a simple flower such
And dinners we share must be Dutch
If you seek she whom you can shield
Others many are in this field

I take but fairly give as well
to those astray within my spell
If you give me joyous freedom
to any ends for you I'll come

Give me your means to my behest
Bring fresh meat, I'll do the rest
If to this promise you'll confess
Then my love shall have no duress"

"O Dahlia, though fair of grace
These many have a trying face
It seems a work too much for me
After all, I'm just a bee

Perhaps your hornet or the mantis
Is better suited of your kiss"
And saying such, his wings a blur
Danced he next to the sunflower

The Invention of the Dare *(Sep 2022)*

Deep into the seas of Reld
There lay a goblet held
The hand which path'd hath cooled its wrath
Its final foes all fell'd

Under low lies cobalt tide
The folk, from men aside
They drank the lust of those most just
To grow their bonafide

The stares most pale through sunny night
Did have both claw and teeth that bite
The shining caves swallowed both knaves
And gods testing their might

One such fool did make the way
To those cheery caves one day
The Relded folks, their flames on stokes
At this morsel were gay.

Meaning of the Poem (in Taran's words)

1st stanza:

It means that there was a creature - something sinister - perhaps a man, perhaps something ethereal, that submerged itself into the caves. The caves themselves are called Reld, so said creature immersed itself even deeper into the seas of the caves. It holds a goblet- the goblet contains the emotions that it still has. It symbolizes the torch the creature holds to its final self, what it is at that current moment after centuries of change. The hand which path'd mean the hand which, by its path, held the goblet- essentially a different way of saying the hand which held the goblet, i.e. the creature itself. It had drunk this brew of the emotions it had- the emotions it thus thought it required to survive, and after such a period in the seas had cooled its wrath. It was the last of mutual foes- dozens of enemies killing each other- but it had emerged, if not victorious, but alive, the last one. Such damage affected it- turned it into something that didn't have characteristic emotions that defined sentient creatures- turned it into a monster incapable of the emotions it might have once had.

2nd stanza:

In the caves of Reld is the cobalt tide (blue ocean) of the caves. From that creature that was mentioned in the first paragraph spawned the Relded folk- people or a population that was aside from men (different from normal humans). The lust of just people- the things that righteous people desire or want is authenticity- glory in purity and the right thing- that is their lust, unlike the lust of normal folk, which is greed and vanity. The Relded Folk drank this lust- consumed it and used it for their own to grow their bonafide- to make themselves seem more friendly and cheery- the word seen in the final stanza. As we can see, they are appearing to be a form of siren- a type of monster that lures unsuspecting people in by appearing welcoming and amicable, and devours them. They used that lust (here: righteousness) to make themselves seem nicer to the outside world.

3rd stanza:

On a sunny night, obviously, the night is bright. A pale stare is light-coloured- characteristic of mysterious stares. However, usually they shine through dark nights, to make themselves contrast. A pale stare in a sunny night (a day, for practical purposes) is invisible, essentially implying that you couldn't actually see any stare at all. The sentence inverts itself to make the stares seem more sinister. Coupling that with the next line, we see that the owners of the stares had teeth and claws that scratched and bit. For effect, it means that, as the stares were invisible and undetectable, one wouldn't realize the fate of one's demise until it was too late and the claws and teeth acted. The next line says that the shining caves- as in the caves with sunny nights- swallowed (i.e. manoeuvred such peoples into coming inside) both knaves, as in dullards and weaklings, and gods that tried to test their might. It tempted, attracted, swallowed and ultimately catalysed the death of both the weaklings and gods with much power but not enough power, who thought the Relded folk to be a pushover.

4th stanza:

Now, we see the essence of the name of the poem. One fool made the way to the cheery caves. As we see, the caves appear friendly and placid from the outside- proof of the workings of the bonafide so exhibited in the 2nd stanza. The fool is a fool because they were dared to enter the cave and come back out, perhaps by their peers. The poem intentionally supposes to Perseus, Jason, and many other heroes of different myths in different cultures, where they take foolishly dangerous and deadly missions as dares and, by a miracle, succeed. This poem talks about the more likely and more realistic outcome, where such a person is a fool for taking a dare, perhaps for proving his worth or bravery, or simply as a brash denial of the existence of carnivorous and catabolic creatures in the caves, showing that he is convinced by the Relded folk's bonafides. Such a person is a fool for this reason as the Relded folk prey on such a target. When he enters we see that the Relded Folk had their flames ready to cook (i.e. on stokes) and at this treat or bit of food were joyant and satisfied.

Cherry Butterflies *(Nov 2021)*

Wraith'd did sing in black the white
To be gone, to come, to purse sorrows of keeps
the joyaunce- it's back again shall see mine eyes- or so one curs'd the light

She who veiled the night in the tempest- She of many wombs come born
Alit did order through her wane- none sorry for her bane
that cursed bright light that spawned the thoughts
devils made in their forgots
the terrible she, the Moon!

The arboretus made for eyes- that sought the Sun, not pine folk's rum
That white filly must banish hell- to take its place and face her knell
But in the catacombs of pale and rich and bundled flores

Blaz'd to light by sunny tides
The green and dappled dapper vines
Perfume sparked the smouldered air- whipp'd the sense to wild affair
The valley soar'd on blossom boats- the white and red lilies
Did meet the feet
Defeated defeat
And made new pasts for sins untold- waters dearth'd of ugly cold

Upon the blossoms rode their lords; they tread through air and sea
The flowers, creeks, and, lakes and ponds
To this land, no man had bonds
And such that butterflies that rode their cherries to cloudless abodes
Were kings
To lose to another wild foe
A fool's thought- for they had no woe
And whence the sun went to the girl, Daphne, with her black locks curled
While winds wept their deep love-swept sighs
More than fear and other lies
His stomach had cherry butterflies

A Beggar of the Sun *(Feb 2022)*

T'was he, the child old of him
The cursed whose mother had dwelt less
on land and sky, from ear to eye
Seen less and heard but wisps

T'was such this child that illed the sun
Broke the heart of he who had none
This child hath a small body
But his mind lives amply

Doth summer tides did shine the blues
The sandy coves of jay and day
And twitter through after wild nymphs
The satyrs did chase slow

In such joyaunce the blues did part
the whites were told to far depart
the honey did catch all fillies
that darted through their trees

the goats did run for fear of leer
they'd wait a day to catch their fey
his Brightness gloried out in search
of she who made him dazed

the fillies cantered round the Sun
their auburn locks did snare those eyes
their petty shawls and rich bosoms
that softened in his sunny fleece

the sun did stride through nymph and girl
as silks and dress were cast to side
he hath be swept- not by their charms
the prurience saved for she, for she!

Traversed he past rivers and creeks
where many a glowing filly gleam'd
the stallion searched for his mare far
his nightmares circling beyond the dark

"His lascivious would like to come
and spend a cove with me, just me!"
cried nymph of tree and rock and flore
the flittering bodies on the forest floor

They hunted close to his divine
His shoulders shone in virile prime
and soon, there was quite many a girl that
lay from his ornate arms to
the lean legs that were his grand steeds
bred of pure blood of his creed

the luscious raptures of these creatures
made no mark in his eyes which
did glean with pride and calling lust
to find she for whom his heart fussed

then saw her did his eyes, knees that weak
did turn from their stolid teaks
She with green eyes, black locks and
the brooke waters on her long limbs

the form of his up in the sky
did bronzen things to her eyeryes
His golden shade upon her chest
did silence all the rest

the fillies, skittish, ran to trees
that bore their kith and ancestries
the sun and she were quite alone
his nerves did turn to brittle stone

His form saw she, then took her shawl
draped it, questioned, "Who be thou?"
The sun did blink then questioned back
"Thee glory knows not of my glory?"

"The sun I am on this fine day
but I may change if you should say
I crafted fey, the day and does
I am the mighty Apollo!"

"I mayn't become one of thou house
why need thou with for me?
the fillies skittered round thy feet
quite pleased they'd show their fingers too!"

"Why doth thou wish a nymph to wed
thine wish may quench with a goddess instead
I wilt not come with or for
for reasons that I keep afore"

The sun did weep and fell in half
He reached to touch her ebon strands
"I beg of thee, my heart doth ache
do not banish me in wake."

Daphne smiled tart and sweet
She acknowledged his defeat
"Oh, what a tale to tell, what fun!
"I've made a beggar of the sun."

Ayeloie *(Jun 2022)*

I traipsed through trees and glades that shown
of deepest green and winsome glean
that shock'd me from the tips of ears
to cherry butterflies that swarmed
and cackl'd in my vacancy
and far out and up to trees
that mock'd my dappled radiance

"To run would be as knives that sailed
to pierce mine hard and pull my hairs
my foe be he who blessed the nymphs
with fecund, swift vitality
but words I use that naught do show
the vigour of your undertow
which sweep'd me off my feet to you."

"The sea is much the better of you
for he stays to his waters true
and knows the hand upturned to mean
another nymph is yours to woo
and as she coquets coy and wild
I dash out of your eyes and mind
And thus am free to dance my dance."

"But My Lady, do please not go!
my sight will cloud and fog my sense
the crops that bathe in my glory
will dry and turn to barren stalks
and grassy prairies turne'd to rocks
will curse your name to deepened smoke
Daphne left to rot and soak!"

"A hell that lilted my flowers
that burn'd me in the cold showers

such a fate next to your hand
seems plenty that I could just stand
Your hips and lips and beauty seems
to come from Venus She, who too
who like you, thinks that that's enough."

"I weaken'd my frame heaved in gold
my tears did flow as summer rains
though I do not call rain not tide
for I, the sun could win the hand
the game was never lost by I
who was equipped with all that men
did dream of in their heady gins."

"Whence you seize to play this game
to play it not till death you face
upon the day you learn loyalty
you may wed one with beauty as me
though that will surely take the years
that creatures like you will not see
even Hera my face fears."

The lightnings arced and and chopp'd the skies
Daphne screeched as her limbs grew
the sudden rains did leave the dew
upon her newfound leavers and roots
and the sun, like a mirage
the clouds hidden like camouflage
as I suffused in silent sound.

"You stand to honour victory
for those who show virtues will see
that beggars get just dirt and grime
the greatest mayn't give them much time
and you will love and live in me
You showed me my blighted Chutzpah
A forth I hail you, Ayeloie!"

Eldamy Grove *(22 Apr 2021)*

Whilst most they call me Hattie Cutt
All know naught my title
Neither shall you, so call me Cutt of Hattie
For its far more romantic a name

In smoggy Bath, the filthy city, the Machines did all the work
So urchins such as my little guardians could wager forth no price
As a little creature of sharp bones, it was quite rancid a place
Not safe a haven but instead a changeling district of hell

Oh, but my Grove! My gorgeous Grove!
The graves of the Eldamy dead
The Eldamy name was crushed so long
Before even the Fey did bleed

I knew not worry or mortal harm and why my guardian held my hand
Whenst tall, thin elven suits that wrapped Fey went through Mest
Mest, the ghastly alleyways, the huddled broken death!
The place I knew as vile peril, except my Eldamy Grove!

Mest where all the Fey and fowls went after the Glad
The wreak of life that maladicted the all, last, every my kind!
I less knew this at the age, when I graced the Grove
My quaint, sweet, home of stone and green among the steam of Bath

Once when I played my life changed strings, a day of fate's mercy
A High Elf came strolling through, slighting the Eldamy Grove
Seen me, said he, "Oh pallid child! What gives light to the sky?"
I spoke as my mouth thought, careless! "Elpis, the hope around dread"

Smiles he bestowed upon this, held out a hand to I
"What did your mother tell you, say?" He asked, agleam of warmth
I pursed mine lips, then said from mind, "The Great Orator of the Air!"
He beckoned me, did he to come, to sail away from Mest.

I turned back where to my damp home, my guardians trundled on
I was the pain, a burden, one more mouth they to feed
Oh, horror, had not I been in my Grove, never would I to leave!
A horrid prospect, and in all truth, Eldamy Grove freed me.

He took a metalled feather from the innards of his coat
A twirled décor of his sly finger and what a swirl of flutters!
He whisked me far and long away, to grow up near Bath Senate houses
To learn the might and corruption that was the politics

Oh, what a glistening world Bath was, whence one saw just the top!
Huge hovering structures, bronze soaring galleons, agoras on the ground
And the 'coated elf' as my whisker was called; what addled items had he!
Smiling brass owlets from ruins of the Glad, like grim things, made them glad.

Hattie Cutt, or p'raps just Hats, as all High knew me then
I knew though of the Mest and that Bath hadn't bathed in several clocks
Yet I strove hard; I rose the ranks! I came upon Senate lunch
And my senate hall did palimpsest the poignant Eldamy Grove

My Senate Hall, where all knew me! Hattilvana Cuttorice !
The changeling waif who ruled the hall, who came from the under, Mest!
Eldamy Grove was gone, gone far; my Senate was my mark
Yet foolish I did lust for more, *a pilot*, the great honor!

I flew through quick, and soon I was, the ace of Bath Corral
Fit finally to steer his craft, The Orator of the Air!
I clambered into his vast ship, a zeppelin forged of steel,
It shadowed Bath, the bronzen city, metal birds ticking through the air

And Oh! Yet again it came, the whittle brush! The paint on used canvas
My beautiful Eldamy Grove, the start! It all began right there!
Yet cockles deep and lost long ago, the Senate Hall instead
Then that, too, gone by high clouds! Command the ship of the Orator!

The greed I got whilst doing so, I aspired quite too far!
Shouldn't I to be the next Orator? I must dispose of the Old!
Merely schemes, before he scuttled in, and threw me off his blimp
The thought Hattie Cutt chose as she fell to her death, *All because of one Eldamy Grove.*

Socrates *(Dec 2019)*

As yet does this world hold promise to any of its kin?
What do I see, my own followers, jeering back through the din!
Does my lament hold any element at all?
For the poison ere forth, nothing can be done, and soon will I fall
Brutal may be it, just hemlock grants alone
The time enough for scribes to carve my last words onto bone

If only wise Solum's kingdom this was, Oh, do I gain!
Where liquors of rums and death serums brought along one's bane
When one sinks into slumber at rest, blessed is he!
The devil claims his soul underneath, though no fee!
The worst of condemned rogues, at the waning day
Lay weary heads down, feel a prick, souls away!

Ne'er more do I satisfy by harbouring 'est visions
Hemlock is unforgiving, below my skin, boils the crimson
My life, like a ship, dock'd at earth's harbour
The ropes unty'd, the captain says, "Set sail for the devil's grandeur!"
Who be the captain? Why none but I!
As the devil reels my ship in, I await his orders to die
How charming he be, much like a flower I know
But pretty things often conceal, arrow and bow
His petite little noose inches up to crack my soul
I will soon be member of the cunning devil's bowl

"Make haste, I say!" my captor cries, holding the bowl of death
I am jerked to back, his scowling face, looms before my breath
"What care, have you?" vexed do I say,
"For my flight from this world makes all of you gay
Does poison pay regard, for wisdom flowing to the loyal
For who be source of wisdom, why, hemlock has mack'd me toil!"

"Understandably, I understand, but do now stem this flow
Wise may be it, for it must be a seed that knowledge sows
But to my ears, it's quite a bore
The words one finds in preachy lore."

A common feeling of common humans arises to my lips
The cognitive defence we feel so bare runs to my fingertips
My lips are caught by none, but I, as I remind myself with a great sigh
That such emotion was not worthy of being felt by one like I!

But truth there be, in that man's say
What use are such anecdotes by dusk of day?
I have been abandoned by all of this world
Humanity has driven straight through me its sword
"You right as ever are, here never you fell in line"
"So, I come to invite you along to the world that is mine."

And nigh by me sat an angel, as queer as queer can be
Neither beautiful nor ugly, jaunty nor sullen, rich nor poor to see
But in his eyes, I saw none but I, smiling right back at me
And I knew she wanted nothing from me but showed me how Death should be
"Would you be Death?" I asked of him, my voice neither joyful nor sad
And his next words had more sight than any eyes ever had

Death is not a giver of boons; he doesn't give help in dire need
She is not the one to be praised for instilling life into every seed
Death is merely a mirror for all, with their life is it should be
But life is never as life should be, then what fun would be there, for thee?
Truth you do speak, of course, your life was quite indeed unfair
So that is why I offer to you in my hall a chair
made of white marble and silver, decked with roses and heather
quite fitting indeed, for the heart that will rest on it is pure as a feather
I give you what others have naught, and no need to roll the dice
A seat of honour inside my realm, join me in paradise!

Joining her I ascended up to sky, looking down the world I saw
And just one pang of guilt I felt marred my feeling of awe
Though evil, heartless and cruel they be, filled with cunningness
In the end they all deserved, to receive this Honour's bless

The Girl of Dragon Cove *(11 Oct 2020)*

Do you know the girl who sits alone on dragon cove?
It is quite a tale, not many do know, it happened ages ago
On a rock high in the cove, does she sit, where the dragon was once in his den
Overlooking the ocean and calling many a ship, in her eery haunting siren

Her story is lost, but her presence is not, for many a boat has gone astray
The sailors staring at the girl while she sings, steering their boat into the bay
They don't look down, a fatal whim, and there they meet their end!
Their ship gets caught in the clamping jaws, the girl and her rocks their send

And still she sings, not caring forth, for the deaths of those beneath
For she calls as though she wants a treasure, which none yet have bequeathed!
But not many know, what her treasure is, and why she sits in the raging storms
Why she sits in dragon cove, a place where they says men's souls are torn

But I do know, and I shalt tell you, for then you'll understand
For how silver-tongues are keys to death, or fate in the cove's black sand
So I ask you, do you know, the Girl of Dragon Cove?
It is quite a tale, not many do know, it happened ages ago

In the distant land, of cloud forests, and walls of great stone and brick
Of those chessboard creatures, and circular hats, and eves with fog so thick!
Back then when, in western Earth, Rome was soaring free and strong
While in the misty East, our Girl of the Cove, was of a village with forests along

Why such a dreamer, one never saw, her head full of bright colour
And visages of glory and ancient soldiers riding to honour
In her small village, her people were happy as they could be, but they were poor
And those absent copper coins did naught to fill the girl's vibrant lures

But her little village was quite an omen, to those within and out
For nigh the village, on a sky-rimmed mountain, was the prison of the dragon
For a thousand years or so ago, the gods had chained all of these mighty serpents
To the tops of mountains above the clouds, where they thrashed in briny repent

And of course, the girl, and her head with lore, she longed to see the dragon!
A glorious beast, of beauty untold, and this was the dragon of the sun!
The brilliant scales, flashing as they behind pulled, the chariot of the sun thane
And drove it across the pearled sky, and brought to the village light and rain

And this girl, her head in fantasy, had used their family's savings one day
And bought a little goldfish from a traveller, so the Koi and she could be gay
Oh, what a rant, her father gave, and she felt as hopeless as could be
She decided she would tame the dragon, reeling above, and let her father see

So that night, she stole away, and took with her her fish,
And started the forbidden climb that led to the top where lay her fondest wish
She ascended, through the night, until at dawn,
she broke to the top of the mountain
And there lay, like a glowing star, the dragon of the eons forgotten

The girl walked around, her eyes shone with lust and greed
And she walked around and marvelled at the chains and the rapturous beast
Then the dragon reared and wailed in anguish, its lips in a human leer
Oh! Really so strangely human you'd think and
thus sympathy eclipsed the girl's fear.

She called to the beast, "O' brazen serpent, how forth hath thou here?"
And the dragon cried, for he had a voice, and he spoke in melodic sneer
"Hath lost to the world, for the Gods were afraid, of my solitary vicious state
So they cast me here to this clouded peak, for time to decide my fate".

And in such a plaintive voice he spoke of his
trouble and tears came in the girl's eyes
"And once for a thousand years, one may ask of me a boon, should they
dare to here rise
And as disharmonious or preposterous it may be, it shall be matched!
And on any other tide should one parry forth my rocks my thirst for
blood shalt be quenched"

Realizing what the beast implied the girl shrank back in alarm
The dragon heartily guffawed and cackled, saying,
"Today I shall do thou no harm!
So little girl of your Koi and silks, what treasure do you seek asunder?"
And as he spoke his wings flapping and beating
called wind and claps of thunder

The girl thought a while, While the dragon recited tales of its pure past life
And so silvery was his gleaming prose, soon her mind was devoid of strife
She called, "O Sun Dragon of centuries old, scribed in only your memory
For my ultimate wish I call thou to be free,
to fly over the rivers Red and the Dee"

With a sunlit burst, the chains snapped off and the dragon soared up in
the morning sky
But he didn't far get, before he plummeted back,
crashing next to the girl with a sigh.
For Chinese Dragons, they cannot fly,
the Gods did place on their foreheads a dome
A sphere of gold smaller than a palm, but heavy, holding them to the tomb.

But wait! One thing hast not spoken by the cunning beast:
Those shackles must always carry one being at least.
And now that place was reserved for the girl
But one more thing the dragon wanted from her.

"I've wanted to soar over moors and lakes,
But this ball on mine head keeps me on the earth's makes
I should shake thine hand and be your own
Should you relieve me of this dome".

And with real sadness was laced his voice and the harshness of the Gods
She spoke," Canst thou do it? For your own well, with your sharp clawed rods?"
"Tis my curse, little girl! Hath those heavens been cruel indeed",
And then with a swoosh of the girl's glimmering knife,
fell down the golden bead.

The dragon purred with indulgence and excitement
The girl's eyes flashed with visions of contentment
She'd descend from high, down to her village, the sun on her dragon's coat
Sparkling like pristine plates of gold, while she on his back would gloat.

Then her eyes still gleaming with rapacious malice,
She flew back, her arms in the dragon's chains fist
The dragon shrieked with effacing glory
And the Gods watched from their heavenly storey.

The dragon flieth to the world of stars, his teeth glistening with light
And he devoured the Gods, finally full, while none could put forth worthy fight.
He sank back down, his vengeance razed, and went down to her chains
She wailed to him, "O great snake of old, why hath thou those Gods slain?

"And sentenced me to thine own locks, for what to come of me?"
The dragon intoned with wily gait, "Oh girl, This trouble is for thee
Thou shalt never more trust serpent or man and resolve your own fate
Lest such like this might capture thou to be left to condensate

"But perhaps one day a long time away, I might come back to you
For this is my turn to see the world while man takes my peak of doom
I might return and take thine chains to exchange seats of this peril
And let thou be free to go and live out their dreams as to their own will."

And leaving the sobbing girl behind, he sailed away and was gone
And trailing as he glided forth, he sang his phoenix song
The girl heard, and since, not a moment without, she calls the beast with his ode
And still now she sits in the cove, singing the tone, waiting for the dragon's return.

So do you know the girl who sits alone on dragon cove?
It is quite a tale, not many do know, it happened ages ago
On a rock high in the cove, does she sit, where the dragon was once in his den
Overlooking the ocean and calling many a ship, in her eery haunting siren

The Queen's Garden *(Sep 2020)*

'Ere forth a tale of heavens old
Of times that to man are mystery
An age that tells of beings vile
Ruling the world before history

Long before the reign of pompous man
There lived the race of giants
The Thoons they were called, the killers of fate
A devil the Queen of these tyrants

The Queen's Garden the Earth was called
Beyond its gate lay chaos
In the Garden grew the first life and death
Little cockroaches she called us

The gate to the Garden manned by mountains
Or Thoons, whichever you prefer
And the little creatures had no salvation
From their miserable lives to serve

Out near the gate sat a bloody tower
Where the dreadful Queen held court
Those cockroaches and enemies
Would unfairly subject to sort

One fateful day of cruelty and evil
Was one that condemned the innocent
Hungry daughters of the Silver-tongued God
While the Queen's claws their backs bent

The two sisters were kept in an audience room
Tried in a court open to the gate
Far above in the devil's tower
Sat the Monarch and her killers of fate

Taken one at a time they tried the first sister
A daughter of the Silver-tongued God
Accused of such a heinous crime
Stealing bread from between the Queen's claws

For then was a time that bread was rare
A luxury for members of the Garden
The mortals below, on the floor of the Garden
Were devoid of such pardon

The little creatures were meant to scavenge
To scrounge for a daily meal
While the Thoons above devoured cakes and cream
Their hunger making those below kneel

The brave young woman and her sister
Were hungry, hungry, their stomachs curled
A satisfied body was a boon
And so their plan unfurled

She begged for forgiveness; the mighty Thoons,
Guards of the Queen's treasure horde
Were better at their jobs than she thought
And caught them at the points of their swords

The Queen in her seat was not pleased,
Nor her Gallery, Thoons and jury,
So, on the daughter of the Silver-tongued God
They unleashed their fury

From high above, in the golden throne,
The Queen and gallery, with her painted claws
Upon the daughter of the Silver-tongued God
Threw rocks, scraping the girl raw

The barrage went on, while her sister screamed,
The Queen cackling as she did
The daughter stood while the rocks chopped
At peace with her eyes at their lids

As the time flickered by, the rocks dropping
Never ending from the tower's face
And finally the daughter, wounded and tired
Fell, dying in her sister's embrace

The girl wailed, the sound echoing
Around the gate and towering rods
For grief washed over the other daughter
Of the Silver-tongued God

The Thoons at the ground, seized the dead body
And without haste flung it out of the gate
The daughter of the Silver-tongued God
Stared, eyes blazing with fiery hate

The Thoons came back with axes high
The Queen gave her final word
The head of the child of the Silver-tongued God
Was to be met by axes blurred

The beautiful child, her head held high
Neither fear nor grief on her façade
Only eyes with steely resolve as expected from
The daughter of the Silver-tongued God

The Thoons grabbed her and hauled her to
The dais set for the act
The beautiful girl saw the Queen's Garden
And the void of inky black

The child looked up to the Queen above
And said with an icy smile
'we had your bread and our stomachs are full
And yet you're no less vile'

The Queen screeched with fiendish rage
And her hand went down to close
The axe in the hand of a mighty Thoon
Went to the child's head

And from the blood of the courageous girl
Came a glorious, beastly flame
The Queen's Garden it devoured with hunger
Ravaged by the fire untamed

The satanic Queen and pitiless Thoons
were consumed by the ravenous blaze
The floor of the Garden, the sky, the walls
were burned to a dust and razed

Out from the ash came an orange sea
The garden drained of water
And tumbled through from the endless desert
The Silver-tongued God's daughter

The Aleithyran Tayle *(Sep 2020 – Jan 2022)*

And doles through and world unearthed far
This one lay cracked in the shimmering mist
A fabled lore of dusty straits
And pining silver lights

Oh, several leagues down the way
One would find a paradise of mote
And riddled crows and burdened smoke
And dark and light afresh

A realm set long to milded crest
With doubled wisps of the same
A mountain here and another here
Gilded to the invert

And a greeny fall and waters atwinkle
And ruptured sores of lust
Did wait there alay for one to come and seed
The sanctity of destruction

But this strange and blazened world
Knew not of one gone there
And left, so long, quite long ago
Enough for his footsteps to ghost

The Aleithyran Forrest, this doomscape was called
With Sloths like sloths, and Birds like birds
And those who liv'd in-air and in-shimmer
They did wonder how they were alit

For such a place ne'er could be real
Unless reality was so fickle
For things don't work elsewhere, succeeding in the Forrest
Would have some questions for it

The sundered praires were darkly night
While glowing alabaster, were the cliffs
Ashined with their pearled and blithed light
Trilling a clashing bang of sea

Where did it source, to be so bright?
No sun could be seen in the sky
Yet those shining rocks and bristly bones
Did never fail to smoulder blare

And in this dapper horrifia
This madness of a place
Shone sky of red and sea of green
Swirling far apart and near

And the first of its kind
The Aleithyra
Of untamed beauty
And stalled death

This hidden world vented long and far
To never be gone by man or star
A loop did await one who sought solace
Death of scopes and violent life

A murky dawn and twistled ferns
And jungle thick with scorned limbs
And that greeny fall and waters atwinkle
Did forever confuse the blight

Down the cliffs, the mighty cliffs
In the turquoise sea
There groaned and churned a twisting whirl
A mighty turn of sea

And far down there from the dark prairies
The first one did fall through
What he saw, cannot be said
But returned he smarter than before

The beautiful Aleithyra
This dual world and swirling sea
Hid vanquished burdens and corded ties
And taxed blocks to foresee

Should one go to Aleithyra
They would know the most
It sat in lost confines of gods
Meant never to be disturbed

In that swirl lay human greed
For one who went would want
Everything, and more, and more
And more and more and more

Those sloths like sloths did know of this
And tarry'd far from the churn
They were smart and smarter still
Than the strongest of the men

For greed is best that is left alone
And those who chanced on Aleithyra
Sailed like rain through, and got the greed
And set stone their demise

And spit from the depths down to below
The other side of the world
And world pauses and ryded mules
Was one to confined

To stuck one there on the mountain
Evermore to wait for one more
For that place must hold one person
The throne of Aleithyra

'cept one might questly want a throne
Though this throne was despised
A curse of sorts and every type
Saddened of mite and curls

But from there could one look
Over the plains and cliffs
The wholity of Aleithyra
Captured before the mist

And groves of stars and marionette strings
Did pull through the time
And once man perished the cycle looped
And Aleithyra started once more

And if you had seen as luckily as I
To see but not the whirl
Then you would feel that it was quaint
A fancy for the gods

And once you tread into the whirl
We might take you as lost
For none who go do back come forth
And are instead drawn dead

Then this tayle will cycle past
And as all will come to pass
So I beg thee, when you enter
To keep many these in mind

Altera Naenia - 2

A dotted streak did run between
The above and the below
Where petty qualms like gravity
Were banished from the tayle

The turquoise water did no end have
No bed onto to toil
And across that fabled fickle line
The same was on the other side

And those brighty cliffs of dandy blithe
Well, the same was said for them
For these worlds were meant for themselves
And themselves alone would do

Down to the sloths and birds and falls
And rocks and trees and caves and hills
That dust, that light, that darkling sky
And too the muttering of the air

Every these were doubly cast
A world to set wrought twice
And like evil and greed these worlds were forged
For twins they were since then to come

as here does as there does
As there roars as here roars
For when this land be the same both sides
Where could a foul spawn forth

One might say it was cided cords
Marionettes dangled by whom?
And agree I would for this order place
Was perfecter than luck.

So what was the knife in the shining dream?
The unsaid but implied threat
What locked man out of this hidden gate?
For it was a gate but to where?

Only those meant to be could really be
For their doubles balanced the scale
For every sloth this side a doppler gnawed
The twin of his twigs there

Should halvely bodies taint one side
What indeed would occur?
Where to did the waters gate
And how of the first walker?

I would assure you with full candor
"We're not meant to know"
But I would not aspire to be like the walker
Seeing his stormy fate

Tales Saltus – Tales of the Forrest-3

he roared and reared and shrieked for his own
the torpid flush was his to ravour
those barky sticks of mighty valour
none could match the Forrest

those in the Forrest enjoyed and lived
those outside were green
but the Forrest was a knife of death which
only animal wisety could protect

the shrieking creature howled and mauled
sliced the yellow trees
the red dawn glimmered deep in his eye
there was something wrong

red blight wasn't such to be seen
it didn't change nature
the carpet of clouds was playing wrong
it wasn't supposed to happen

the sloth below did crawl and scratch
catching the little rodents on the bark
he pulled the mice like tarot cards
and tossed them dead to side

still he wealed and gnoded forth
pulling down the tree itself
the stormy sky tightened and bled
the red seeped into the fold

then quite haughty akin fate
did send a curse to the ghost
a forked gasp of abysmal light
did slice through the darkly night

the sky was a second not black but red
the flash burned out the eyes
the sloth writhed and wailed under the tree
the yellow carcass draped on his legs

the bloody tint in his eyes did clear
once again his docile colour
he wailed in sorrow at his sad plight
for he knew not how he came to it

should those surrounding silent Forresters
look but once at the sky with keenity
they'd see no more was the sky red
but it's normed darkly night

they watched from trees and holes and ground
at the poor little sloth trapped under the tree
until in a while, he no more gasped
and the creatures went on with their lives

Fabulas Caverna – tales of the caves-4

Et rotored cliffs and sliced cut clay
The terracotta slits of careen
The red, the orange, the eddled twinkle
Ne'er failed to feast my taste

And flen out of the crying face
Of the cliffs and the clay paints
Were gorged out eyes of catacombs deep
Their tears gone with the eyes

Might once they weeped a languid stream
But one's hard to tell in Aleithyra
Their eyes ran dry a minute ago or
Before time knew even itself

A place ought wet that's dry as scorn
Should not be a fancied desire
Unwrought things before they happened
Were wrought and twisted inside

What'nt to fear of caverns from tears
Tears dropped from the walker's eyes?
It canst to be said that the walker was first
That he was life and to live was he

For those sloths and timid forrest cloids
Would beg their conscience to differ
But life to think and want and want
And want and want was his

Wont to say how the eyes came there
But there they were to stay
Inside one felt the walker's feel
It could madden a priest to bereave

For what be insight than sight itself?
The eyes show how'sth a thought thinks
the ambition and lattied whorls
Of layers of the mind

A commoner's eyes mightn't be worth much
A voyage of uninterest most
But the walker who'd walked and seen great trails
His eyes would sear the sockets of one's own

Again I beg thee not to enter
The Aleithyran caves or Forrest
Or hill or throne or island at all
Must'nt you seek bleak end?

The Avian Symphonaiae *(06 May 21)*

Enter you the Valla hall? To dance, perhaps sing, or jest?
This be the hall of the Avian – He shuns all but the best
So come you forth and give your act – Oh, glimmer your pretty eyes
The Valla ball, the dance, concert! Will take the stars and rise

The Avian may want you to play a fool – or act a meek unworthy tool
But once you enter the Avian's domain, you're his to feed and scold and train
To Blackbird and the Whistler – you are nothing but a weakly cur
But they admire each own things, keep thought when you enter their rings.

May you desire a tragedy? A terrible poignant lear,
The Skylark acts pale incessant – he treats irony as gold
Now whence the lark's the head of show – you'll invoke pathos and your tears
The audience weeps; you bow offstage; you will be his to mould

The drama o'er centuries fold, the lark muttered in the minds
Of Poets, Wrights, helms and kings, he twiddled them in ways he could find
The Skylark trills ere, morns of forth, of Scots and mountains Swiss
They truthfully are cries of despair, and not chirps of bliss

Mayn't you desire a death by tears, the Blackbird gives your quest
He deals in lore and playing cards – from saphahs east and west
And dappled steeds riding to forth – and fey dancing in the leaves
And mooreland creatures in the medieves – and dank dungeons sans keys.

Of pirates sailing looted crafts – of dragon on cold peaks
And black-eyed imps burdening war – of snowflakes in skies bleak
The tales of blood, dance, cards and king – the tarot gods avast era
The Blackbird's whispered in every tale – they're all his plethora

Last come the Whistler, his eerie tune – it keeps loose lips tightly sewn
The Whistler cannot love just death – it must be a cruel last breath
Bestowing trust be a pitied deed – for prize, that friend may make you bleed
Worse than what any foe can do, is what a friend might do to you

Soldiers of any army – their tyrant wields his sword
A mate just might be the king's ear – you shan't be safe from his hive
And if your tongue is not bound tight – he'll nail you to the board
Join the Whistler to know peril – never show him your back, to survive

These three, they make the Avian Trio- a dazzling troupe with bloody perfume
Upon the symphonaiae day they fight – the victor will rule, the others doomed
The play, the ballet, the Vala sonata – who will survive, alive, tell pray ?
If chose you the Blackbird, the Lark or the Whistler, well you might not
live past that day!

The Crell Dock *(26 Apr 21)*

Salty mist did bite my face
As I ran, upturning silk and lace
The Galai market bright with scent
The Crell Dock waiting, with ears bent

Twice many, too close, they grabbed mine heels
Yet, over the bazaar, there rose the keels
The Crell dock was ready, but which boat?
Whomst could I trust, to keep me afloat?

I lunged afore, lost in their eyes
Amongst the Dock and seagull cries
Yet I'd be seen, a moment of rest
Was naught one thing which I had been blest

A leap, a dash, sent me aboard
A grizzly man at me, winced, bored
"Ere much a ferry, cost mine purse?"
"Oh, thoust hath not worry, 'tis not a curse."

His nimble barge did sail me out
Far behind my chasers sagged them louts!
"Hast thee a place to be my friend?"
Whilst words were warm, eyes didn't extend

I narrowed mine own and said, a sly
"Attira, the great fields of rye"
He twiddled a bone through his black teeth
"Aye, vaint a place, but I will, for thee"

My heart did patter, like tempest ponds
The sailor spoke strange and addled bonds
Then from the mist, loomed mirthy gale
Like acts ere forth a pirates tale

A musty ship, vague, out of the grey
Adeck, two men, there joyaunt day!
I flinched at my own captain, asked
"To turn me in, while in the bounty, you basked?"

Then, shocking my sense further more
A gun brought he, shot through the course
Twice rang, then shouts, more under hull
Then all dead, their skin gone bleak and dull

Their ship had lost a dusty crew
To sail ere ever in the ocean dew
"Hast thou gone mad?" I asked, through bliss
"I'm worth a sack, too high to miss!"

Chuckled he, a twisted grin, alit
"Thoust wants to die, so thee throw a fit?
No, mine reasons will be sure to see
Such time will quell your misery"

Then a galleon, black and towering mast
Told me I soon would breathe my last
He cackled mad, but still saner than I
"Why one sack, whenst I can get five?"

Ah! As I was hanged from dark poles
I saw afar the Dock, with eyes dole
If only Attira, or even Docks of Hell
Anything but the Dock of Crell

The Maker of Fools *(Dec 2022)*

Sat I with a company
Of creatures seen not in the light
Tales of that they told to me
That which weakened might

"What makes of a man, clever
His head or heart or ears?
The worth of his tall endeavours
Perhaps his lack of fears"

Said they, to this, when I knew not,
"'Tis grows out of the brain
'Tis treasure that many have sought
And prayed for through snow and rain

But rather one should wish to be
Of rich in mind and rich in heart
But such a soul is rare to see
For mind and heart do live apart"

Next asked was where did come wisdom
Spoke one creature's voice of reeds
And in the throne of her kingdom
I listen as she Leeds

Of many things under the stars
We spoke of, through the raucous crowds
Then our words did go to Mars
And thoughts of its sons proud

But though the currents of this world
And ways to work its winsome waves
Lay clear as day like scrolls unfurled
The thought of love I deemed depraved

For what haste would one break their soul
And seek one who does hurt, not heal?
For treasure that may let heads roll
All just for one's heart's meal?

But my life, short and though plaintive
Has lent a thought from years of sight
That flaws in humans seem to live
Within a lover's loyal light

Whence talking to this sombre maid
I learnt that frame that upholds love
One cannot love who laws evade
For she loved not a dove

(As She Leeds is read now)

And those who claim their clear heads sing
Will, time pray fall chained to the cruel
That which humbles gods and kings
Love, the maker of fools

As She Leeds *(Dec 2022)*

Recited by the creature of Reeds, as she Leeds

"I wandered long enough to rust
I thought not to be prey to lust
But then two men entered my life
And since I never knew such strife

One was all one wished to be
He who possessed every key
The human fault seemed not to lay
In his form, though to none he prayed

But when our paths wound tighter still
And to me, more about him spilled
I learned his might was prey to one
The red and green thoughts overrun

But I loved him never, not me
And he showed not intimacy
For something strange was in his eyes
I knew that he thought love a lie

But soon another man passed through
The gates that I had sealed untrue
But he was different in a way
That made me think t'was a new day

He was charming, glib and sweet
His words lustrous, as sun grown wheat
He was not as cleverness clawed
His talents fell short of the god

But something in his weakling face
Made shallow breath and my heart race
And this I told to my first friend
Though he could not comprehend

And soon the second heart became
A treasure I would fight to claim
And though our times were much of pain
I cared not, for my wits were slain

But long before either I met
Their paths had intertwined and set
The god hated he who caused harm
To she, to me! Within his arms

Though the god's love was for not I
The nights he seen me pour and cry
Did leave their marks deep on the bone
Of he whose feelings most thought stone

But I knew him to be a boy
Of eyes so bright and smiles coy
And his distaste of he I seek
Was founded just on my words bleak

Though t'was not what he understood
The flames of love and its burnwood
He asked of me what do I see
In a man filled with jealousy

I tell myself my love is kind
That I'm not to a madman bind
That wise are turned to fools arranged
And beauty there lay in this change

The god saw not in this beauty
With sorrow gazed my futile pleas
"I thought thou wisdom were above
The fool's maker has mocked you, Love!"

Pledin *(11 Oct 2022)*

A prince did salt a kingdom old
He lived a time when souls were sold
An estate proud the old king built
The heir he left his only guilt

The crown he wore for its rubies
Care not he of the granaries
For future sons his name was sin
But then, all hailed him, ambarin!

When Ambarin, as king, was young
The forest lent a bird that sung
The parrot, to the king flew he
To join his royal coterie

The grand gala to name the bird
Who was fed seeds to most unheard
Was nourished with more gaiety
than if came Earth a deity

Where the regal royals rose
did awake Pledin, from a doze
peering down at him, akin
to children blithe, was Ambarin

T'was Ambarin's deep ambition
To learn the words spilled from Pledin
That these words gone unheard he feared
The fruit trees without at this leered

Upon the days the king held court
Pledin he hoped would retort
to measly cries and alibis
but Pledin cared more of the flies

Then whence once defeated, the king
Sat stroking Pledin's beak and wing
Pledins sober, sombre state
Did force his silence to abate.

Pledin spoke a fractured tongue
All left of deceased times unwrung
But betwixt these wide words of rot
Ambarin heard all that he sought

Morn next, great stones fell from the sky
Read they, the bastard folk must die
The king hung them like toys at fests
But Death took his soul 'fore the rest

More rocks from the heavens crashed
And more peoples were by these slashed
Till fear his kingdom plundered well
With each afraid of when their knell

The mad king was then but shadows
Locked deep in chambers, far from foes
The man muttered madly, aside
The bird who caused the genocide

One day did come stones unheeded
Men turned on he who the bird feeded
Ambarin, his head relieved
Was thankful for his death's reprieve

Pledin from the castle spire
Knew less of men's hatred and ire
He flew to him, who, trees within
Said him to he, "Well done, Pledin"

Meaning of the Poem (in Taran's words)

The poem begins with the introduction to the setting of the world. We are introduced to Ambarin, the son of a great emperor who had paved a mighty kingdom in the medieval world. However, the old king's only ill fate that he left upon his people was his son, the heir. Ambarin wore the crown only for its superficial beauty- he did not care about the granaries and the plight of his people and the management of food.

For the descendant generations, Ambarin's name was a sin to call upon because of his tyrannical rule, but at that time he was hailed as the great king, if only due to the virtues of his father. When Ambarin was a youthful king, the forest, wishing to keep him on his side, gifted him a parrot- a bird that sang and spoke. The parrot quickly flew to the king and joined his royal posse. the next stanza demonstrates how materialistic and disregarding the king was towards his people- he fed his bird grains that the common peasants had never even heard of, and the gala to name the bird was bedecked with the funds that should rather have been used for the betterment of the state.

The bird is named Pledin, which is ultimately the name of the poem. His first morning, he is awoken to Ambarin peering down excitedly at him. Ambarin longed to know the words that Pledin would speak, for he thought (correctly) that a bird bestowed by the forest itself would carry gravity in its words. Ambarin feared that Pledin would speak his prophetic verses when nobody was around to hear, and the fruit trees that stood outside the royal chambers that would tempt Pledin to go fly to them, away from any people, supposedly leered at this. Ambarin kept the bird with him while he dealt with his daily court, and he hoped that Pledin would discern falsehoods in the alibis of the peasants, but Pledin barely paid any attention to these proceedings.

One day, when Ambarin had given up on every hearing Pledin speak, Pledin's perpetual quietness finally forced his silence to cease. Pledin spoke a mix of jargon and random language, but Ambarin heard what he wanted to hear. Whether or not Pledin actually said what Ambarin wanted to hear or Ambarin merely heard what his brain desired in all the cacophony is unknown.

The next day, stones fell from the sky. This is metaphorical to laws and indictments that Ambarin passed, claiming that all Bastard people must die. Ambarin hung all of them, innocent or not, but the last line of this stanza states that Death (the entity) took Ambarin's soul before he took the souls of the innocents Ambarin murdered. However, the line is phrased such that "before" is pronounced as "fore," which may mean that Death took Ambarin's soul then itself instead of and in the place of all the souls of the innocents, sending them all to heaven while taking Ambarin to hell.

Every day, as Ambarin heard more and more from Pledin, more accusations and laws passed against more communities until finally fear was struck into every single citizen of his kingdom, with nobody sure of who would die next.

At that point, the mad king Ambarin was barely seen outside anymore- he just locked himself in his chamber with Pledin, continuously speaking to Pledin and listening to him. every morning new laws would pass that he heard from Pledin, and more people would be killed. The king had gone insane- he refused to be reasoned with or cooperate with another human being.

One day, the people had had enough, and they finally rebelled against he the bird feeded. This means Ambarin in two ways- one, Ambarin was the one who fed the bird, but the bird was the one who fed Ambarin all his illusions and corrupt thoughts. Finally, Ambarin was executed, and in his death, he felt reprieve from the horror he had been living under the manic control of the bird.

Once Ambarin was killed, Pledin unassumingly flew from the castle and away into the forest, blissfully ignorant of the horrors he had caused. The final stanza is interesting, as it refers to an unknown individual in the forest- it may be the embodiment of the forest itself, or it may be someone with a vendetta against the forest- this is completely unknown even to the poet himself. However, this individual clearly trained Pledin to mimic the sentences that he had taught him, and corrupt the young king Ambarin and soil his kingdom.

The poem is an extended metaphor to how the most innocuous and inconspicuous people (in this case, a bird, Pledin) can corrupt the weak of mind and maybe the true cause for depravities to be wrought upon the world.

A Stranger's Help *(Oct 2019)*

Oh, lad!
Why doth thou face maketh sorrow upon this noon pleasantry?
Thou sayeth thy troubles, for a moment beyond cannot I bear without knowing!
Thou shalt now open thy soul, and express thy innest emotion!
What sin casts such shadow upon thy face of youth?
Must it loneliness, or lost bearing?
Thou doth needeth blithe, verily methinks such
Suffer thou will, should not thy troubles vanish
Help can I, to ease thy pain?

Ah, lad!
Thou hast feelt mislaid, right I not?
Thine world doth have suffrages, but thy trouble shalt be quenched
Thinkest not to leave thy suffering malignant
Put I, in thy place to close the wound
For I, hath much experience to help misplaced passions
But I, shalt never bequeath thou my service should not a collateral offer
Worry not and maketh do, son, I ask not kind, but an amicus
Hearest my advice, and forsooth may it grant you

Why, lad?
Cannot thou answer, for what exactly thy suffers?
Thy reason by upon thy tongue, presume I may?
Shalt you divulge the causing, avaunt may its flight!
For what doth thou undiscover thy fullest potential?

Nay, lad!
Not such trifle hampers thy person of youth?
Thine damsel of affection is lost?
This world of unpredictive changes shalt stop not!
For it to pause, our heartbeat dies!
If it sojourns to breathe, our lungs collapse!
Must it tire, our limbs host none potency!

Shalt I continue? Seeyeth my view of our habitat?
Dasen cannot it, so why doth thou find reason to?
Petty faults shalt not halt the universe, and neither thou!

Grasp, lad!
Shalt I bestow upon thy distraught self an insight of this surrounding?
Promise so forth a hear, and I will proceed
Human soul is verily complexed, with several overlayers,
Its mind doth hold sadness, sympathy, jaunt, rage, confusion, jealousy!
I confidently know thy thinkest, but wait, where shalt love be?
Deeply process, doth thou maketh love through these emotions?
Thou stares, ever comprehending, whilst it, looketh back!
Ha! Nought evades thy pervasion! Love doth maketh of every!
Our society, is none but a nutshell within itself, unfolding amongst perception!
Thine suffrage is pitiful, doubtlessly indeed!
Never for thine personal pity, for your unhinged darling!
My pity falls for thy troubles' unimportance to this mechanic humanity!
Pity for thy feeling of undue gratification towards thine conceited mind!
Shame be upon thy charming exteriority and cunning interiority!
Hast I further provide?

Act, lad!
Thine tongue shall give me answer
What be thy reason?
Why doth thou excuse thyself out of a joyful youth?
Hast thy any reason, to remain in sorrow's bonds?
Naught! For never doth even sorrow itself hath such a reason!

Remember, lad!
Doth thou remember thine little darling?
Her eloquent speech and subtle charm?
I see the joy it brings to thy, but wait!
But if only, the others didn't come, but wait!
Distraught are you, it gleams in thine face, but wait!
Ah, mine utmost regards for my, *humility*
My vast knowledge lends me the answer!

Forget, lad!
Thy shalt do as I say for, I say as I mean
Forgetting yields better than remembrance
Thou and thy darling as yet are not connected
So, when she is lost, should thine soul too be lost?

Present, lad!
Thinkest forth this tale of the gods
Three men stand on a side of a ravine
Wondered, did they how to reach the other side!
The nostalgic has but one thing to say,
'Alexander the great! What a bridge he did make'
The architect is ever so proficient,
'The ravine is shallow on one side; mine bridge shall succeed!'
The visionary focuses on quite a different aspect,
'As would one say, a thousand years further,
when this very tale is told, the grass is greener on the other side!'
The nostalgic re-creates the bridge that spanned once across,
but whereth doth it? In nothing but his mind!
The visionary constructs a bridge, though perhaps cover air and
ground it would had his tools doth existed
The architect constructs magnificence,
ten leagues across, wide even to permit an ark through!
After seventeen days, each crosses his own
Who emerges alive and well?
As is in thine case, the present always holds victory
Why dwell in the past?
Why imagine the future?
Why not cherish the current?

Soar, lad!
Thy can lament so never more
Thou will dropeth thy hardship and rise with extravagance!
Chained hath thou been, depressed into sedentariness
Thy psyche and body must wake!
Thou shalt flieth thy wings and soar to free!

Not more can such problems impair thy gaily self
Suffer never further, lest, thou ignore my preach?
My verdict hast been given, though thou need never makest haste in decision
Thy honour shalt fall thine way or mine?
Before thou thinkest thy choice,
remember ever the help my person hast given thou
Thank, lad!
Thinketh thee of the wonder mine words possess
Dissipate hast it of thine sorrow!
Thou ist grateful, I scan from thy person
Though thou face shows confusion, I see!
Though thou thinkest against, I see!
Though thou remembers, forget too do I see!
And from what do I see? The very thing yours before broken I mended!
Farewell, I bids thee adieu.

Request *(19 Jan 2021)*

There isn't much I ask of you
I've done what I liked before dawn
But this one thing you must please do
Take care of my friend when I'm gone

Food and a home are not what I ask
Those are no problems of his
But what he needs is a hearty scratch
A lap on which to lay his head with bliss

For I'm not here much longer
Maybe I'm gone, or maybe just gone
but rub his back and brush his fur
And make sure that he's not alone

It's sad that he'll miss me
But do make sure please
That in you he sees me
And hopefully more than me

Thoghurstand *(12 Jan 2023)*

In the Rover's cradle sat
Sothiene of the undergrowth
Felt not a sundry wind a flit
The nose he won from the old kings
Demure on the lips of his creed.

This raven he saw on a heath,
The house of his own sword,
The great that paint bled on the wall
Did hold from death who in battles old
Had made the wicked warriors fly

Crimson like a virgin dawn,
The embers burnt the fur of game,
Who hung the candle sticks like art
Skulls from glades seem dark for years
The tiger Tobas of the north.

Sothiene met the blood that wet
And whet the blood – like of those wed
The Tobas gras, the grand gala,
The house he sit, held he who slit
The tepid tiger's Tobas throat

And like a Lion killed at hunt
The Tiger's bloody head was nailed
Above the grim and grimy flame
This manor's master'd earned the name
Trebelous was Thoghurstand!

His father died a league ago,
But Sothiene knew him not to mourn
For a tale learnt Sothiene when once young
Of Thoghurstand's taming of wolves
When in the mutiny of Plaedes

When time was just a cradled boy,
Did Plaedes go up in flames and red
The mines that reap'd the hearts serv'd deep
Had reaped the souls of one two more
And Plaedes was under siege

Whence Sothiene's nation rose from stone
A village made of sticks and bones
Daphodes hung the flags in crest
Did Thoghurstand drive unto Plaedes
To raze those slash'd the ship of love.

And whence to Plaedes, the horses glid
The stones saw many made widows
The aged met a waiting foe
The weary met a waiting friend
No mother met her waiting son

And then did Thoghurstand sail next
To Altas, land of Plaedifell
And all of what a coin could buy
Was brought to Lords and shown to Lands
And Thoghurstand's name bouldered bronze

Once, was told, to Vorfa sent
Did Thoghurstand on a conquest
Make red spring's blossoms bloom so soon
But no fruit was bourne of the spring
But grim mountains of wisdom lost

In Plaedes, Altas and Vorfa three,
The Wolves whose kin had so been razed
Thoghurstand removed their hearts
And in the frantic organ's tears
Did wash away the old year's sins

In such a house did Sothiene sit
Among the game of those who lost
And then the grizzled king stepped out
And into the view of his dead
The clothes he wore hued deep purple

Thoghurstand had killed men many
But many regals to him fell too
And thus the red and blue blood mixed
And it was said that he had not
A stitch of cloth t'was not violet

Such a voice did use the lord
As trembled trenches far in dusk
And of the nature of the guest
Did Thoghurstand ask of the prince
And of the prince's leer saw fear

The majesty of the old sir
Was of that of an old sermon
That poured like falls from him, his form
An ancient creature seen the lives
That angels underwrote in blood.

The underfelt was soft as brush
The world below seen his name long
For Thoghurstand was doomed to die
When time was an adolescent
But he proved to be of the Gods

Did brave Sothiene meet the bear's gaze
And ask of him his aid to war
For the kingdom he ought to have ruled
The lands Thogurstand fought to claim
Had fell to the hands of the Cub

The Tiger's Tobas son was proud,
A man under a golden gown
A tiger child of great fire
A hunger quenched through ravaged lands
Did Daphodes kinsland fall into

A cacophony tide was met
As the grizzled man cut out his heart
And told of younglings of full joy
The waters of their minds like ponds
Of lilies frogs and snake charmers

Not for their thirst Thoghurstand laughed
Not for their frailty the old lord stilled
But if the days Sothiene had lived
Were cut on stone, would serve as too
The count of those Thoghurstand killed.

A sombre face wore the old peer
For he had sworn death in white
The love he had his roses shared
T'was greater than his love for life
The garden he would give his son

But he knew that more than roses
The honor that he gave the king
Should hold sway with the scales of death
And from the pleasure he had lived
Thoghurstand raised to raze.

The Lonely Ruby *(Sep 2023)*

Black and dreary looked the skies
A daring trick above
Final words did fly among
The king's last stand, the Aster men and
The Sun and Lune and Thal
All whose merry married death

The eve sat low in the tide of days
A dune in the sands of fate
Belay the men who weary woke, their flag
Hoisted sunder left 'ere field
The Lord great grim and sombre stood
And gazed the mountains that once laughed

Tholan of the Thallas Pride
The youngest of those left
The thoons ushed all those whose breath'd
Stirred dust from the ashen winds
They feared the soul their king was bless'd
Had withered to a wilted rose

No more thought did the think the Thanes
No more ordered ripp'd their lips
Tholan meandered 'round the camp
The lonely ruby of the spring
The friends he lov'd all banished from
The hell t'would meet the land that followed

Dreams he had of serving well
Of people he bestowed himself
The great black thoughts of honour spanned
And now all those he loved fell dead
A gruesome task to count their names
But his right for his the fault

Tholan caught a quick last friend
A man of Astermen
T'was he smoked a pattering pipe
Right as this sayance etched into
The second stone, a great captain
Yearned to the king

The asterman saw fear the face
Of Tholan had shacked down
"Take a draught, oh lad of luck,"
Did Tholan tender take this word
For once he'd heard of great big plagues
That rose from ill advice

But if the pipe had on his lips
And if the king quenched his morals
T'was canyon in a distant moon
The Lune fell first, the Aster next
The Sun then Thallas last to fall
The Lonely Ruby in the dust